RATS!

'Mum said she'd talk to Dad tonight,' said Sam.

'Well done!' said James, turning his record player down. 'How did you manage it?'

Sam frowned. 'I'm not sure,' he admitted. 'I went on about how rats had changed my life, and how I couldn't live without one, all the usual stuff. I was saving the starving myself for a final assault, but she suddenly went all funny when I admired her shoes, and said she'd talk to Dad.'

James shook his head. 'Strange,' he murmured. 'I know Mum is mad about shoes, but I can't see the connection with rats!'

RATS!

PAT HUTCHINS

Illustrated by
Laurence Hutchins

RED FOX

A Red Fox Book

Published by Random House Children's Books
20 Vauxhall Bridge Road, London SW1V 2SA

A division of Random House UK Ltd

London Melbourne Sydney Auckland
Johannesburg and agencies throughout the world

First published by Greenwillow Books, a division of
William Morrow and Company, Inc., New York, 1989
First published in Great Britain by The Bodley Head Ltd. 1989

Red Fox edition 1991

9 10 8

Set in Times
Typeset by JH Graphics Ltd, Reading, Berkshire

Printed and bound in Great Britain by
Cox & Wyman Ltd, Reading, Berkshire

RANDOM HOUSE UK Limited Reg. No. 954009

Papers used by Random House UK Limited
are natural, recyclable products made from wood grown in
sustainable forests. The manufacturing processes conform to
the environmental regulations of the country of origin.

ISBN 0 09 993190 7

For Sam, who loved his rats:
Treehouse, Spot and Nibbles —
and for Veronica, who didn't.

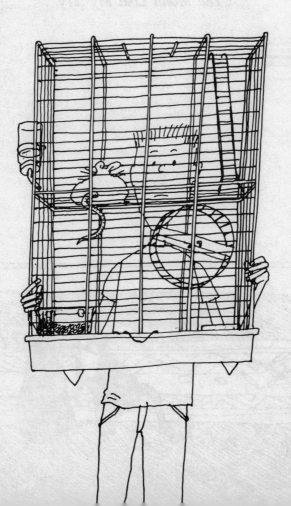

Contents

1
Rats

Sam wanted the rat more than anything else in the world.

He'd seen it in the pet shop on Monday.

It was a soft, pinkish-grey with bright black eyes and a white throat.

Each day, on his way back from school, Sam went into the pet shop to admire the rat, and each afternoon, when he arrived home, he pleaded with his mother to let him have the rat.

He told her how the rat had started to

recognize him and ran to the front of the cage whenever he went into the shop, and how its eyes followed him and gazed sadly after him when he left the shop. What he didn't tell his mother, but told his older brother James, was that he'd bought the rat and told the lady at the shop he would collect it on Saturday.

Today was Wednesday, and Sam, who had been working on his mother for two days, was getting desperate. He thought his mum would be easy. He knew Dad would be more difficult. But his brother James had said that once he'd persuaded Mum, she'd persuade Dad, and if Sam concentrated on Mum, Sam would get his rat.

Sam had Mum cornered in the kitchen.

'But *why* can't I have a rat?' he demanded.

'Sam,' his mother pleaded, 'please don't mention rats again. I've told you a hundred times already why you can't have a rat. The cats will get it. And eat it,' she added, wincing at the brutality of the statement — but she was getting desperate, too.

'It will be in a cage,' said Sam. 'In my bedroom.'

'That's cruel,' said Mother. 'You can't keep an animal caged up all the time.'

'I won't,' said Sam. 'I'll keep my bedroom door closed, and let it out every day.'

'But what if someone opens the door?' Mother asked. 'And Squiffy rushes in? You know what she's like with birds.'

'I'll put a big sign on my door, saying "Keep Closed At All Times",' said Sam. 'Then no one will open it.'

'The cats can't read,' said Mother, pleased with her clever remark.

'And they can't open the door when it's closed!' said Sam triumphantly.

'What if it slips between the floorboards?' Mother asked. She already knew the answer.

'My bedroom's carpeted,' Sam replied. 'All the floorboards are covered.'

Sam picked up his book again.

He knew he was impressing his mother with his newly acquired interest in reading. Sam had never found reading easy, and although his parents had tried every possible way, including bribery, to get him to read, he always found books boring; because by the time he'd worked his way down to the bottom of the page, he'd forgotten what had happened at the top.

'*Rattus, rattus,*' he read aloud. 'Order *Rodentia*. Family *Muridae*. Description: The tail is hairless and covered with rings of scales. The snout is pointed . . .'

Mother, who was delighted that Sam was reading, just wished it was a different book. She knew the book off by heart and secretly suspected that Sam did too. Mother listened to the familiar words. She'd heard them so often she was beginning to chant them in her sleep.

She interrupted Sam. 'I must just pop to the toilet,' she murmured, hoping she could slip away without offending him.

But Sam, still reciting from his book, followed her to the bathroom.

Mother, who didn't really need the toilet, opened the bathroom door. Then, closing it behind her, she pressed herself against the wall, waiting for Sam to go away.

But Sam had no intention of going.

'Listen to this,' he shouted from the other

side of the door. 'It says they make excellent pets.'

Mother gave up and opened the door.

Sam broke off from his reading.

'You forgot to flush the lavatory,' he said.

'How did it go?' James asked, as Sam went into his brother's room.

'She's weakening,' said Sam. 'She tried hiding in the bathroom. I think another day should do it. It's Dad I'm worried about,' he added.

'Once you've got Mum, she'll work on Dad,' said James. 'You've got to get Mum first.'

But Sam thought Dad was worth a try anyway.

2

Suspicions

'What's this?' Dad asked when he came home. He picked up the book that Sam had carefully placed on the arm of Dad's favourite chair.

'It's Sam's book,' said Mother.

'Sam's book!' Dad echoed in disbelief. 'Sam doesn't read! He's got a whole roomful of books he doesn't read!'

'He borrowed it from the school library,' said Mother.

'Good heavens!' Father exclaimed, opening the

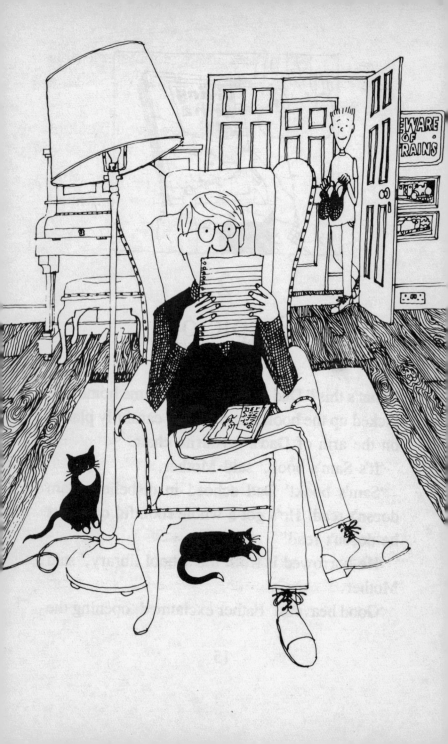

book. 'It's got great, long, unpronounceable Latin words in it. I thought he was supposed to have learning difficulties.'

'Well, he doesn't seem to have any difficulties in reading that book,' said Mother. 'He read the whole thing from cover to cover this afternoon. And yesterday afternoon,' she continued gloomily, 'and the afternoon before that.'

'Ha!' said Dad. 'Pretended to, I bet!'

'No,' said Mother firmly, 'he read it aloud. Very aloud!' she added, remembering the bathroom incident.

'Good heavens!' Father repeated, as a sheet of paper fell out of the book on to his lap. He looked at the neat writing on the paper. '<u>Rattus, rattus</u>. A study of their behaviour.' And written underneath, with subheadings, proper sentences, and no spelling mistakes, was a whole page, all about rats. 'You can't tell me he wrote that,' said Father, handing the page to Mother. 'James must have written it. Look at the writing.'

Mother looked at the writing.

'It's not James's writing,' she said. 'It's too neat. And besides, the spelling's too good!'

Sam, who had heard his father's car arrive and was hovering outside the sitting-room door listening to the conversation, thought it was a good moment to make his entrance.

'Hello, Dad,' he said, kissing his father on the cheek, 'how was the office today?' Then, noticing a slightly suspicious look on his dad's face, added, 'I've brought your slippers for you.'

The look of suspicion deepened and, too late, Sam realized that he'd probably overdone it. 'You look a bit tired!' he added limply, attempting a reason for his generous behaviour.

Dad knew his boys kissed him on his return from work only when they wanted something; usually money.

'How did he know I looked tired, when he was upstairs getting my slippers?' Dad addressed Mother, but fixed his gaze on Sam.

'You sounded tired,' Sam said, as he unblinkingly returned Dad's gaze. 'From upstairs.' Sam's eyes were beginning to water.

'Ah! There's my thesis on rats,' he said, blinking his eyes in relief at the paper in Mother's hand. 'I've been looking for it. I need to do some extra work on sexual patterns. There is so much to learn about rats, especially the *Rattus, rattus* variety.'

Father stared at Sam open-mouthed. 'Is this my son who has remedial coaching in reading and writing?' he demanded of no one in particular. 'Whose teachers are concerned because he's two years behind his age group? This boy who is talking like a walking volume of the *Encyclopaedia Britannica*? What happened?' he asked, turning to Mother.

'He's developed an interest in rats,' said Mother.

Father relaxed. He'd expected an ulterior motive. He'd expected his son to ask him for money. Now he felt guilty, and Sam, sensing this, tried to look modest, intelligent, and a little bit misunderstood at the same time. He even tried to keep the glint of triumph out of his eyes when Father added, 'I shall go to the bookshop tomorrow and find some more books on rats for you. And later,' he promised, 'I'll run a steam train.'

Sam's heart sank. He could never understand his dad's obsession with trains, or his conviction that everyone in the house shared his obsession. But Sam knew that the ultimate sign of approval was when Dad offered to run a train, and Sam needed Dad's approval.

If Dad was happy with Sam, Mum could work on Dad on Sam's behalf.

'Gosh!' said Sam. 'Thanks, Dad!'

'How did it go?' James asked, as he popped into Sam's bedroom to say goodnight.

'Not too bad,' said Sam. 'I left my piece on rats for him to see — he was pleased with the writing;

although I nearly blew it,' he added. 'I overdid it with the office routine.'

'Yes,' agreed James, 'he gets very suspicious if you're too nice to him.'

'I had to sit through a steam-up,' said Sam, 'but that's a good sign.'

James shook his head in sympathy.

'At least it proves you're in his good books,' he said. 'But take my advice, concentrate on Mum first.'

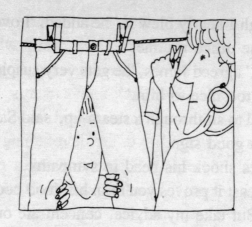

3

More Suspicions

Sam concentrated on Mum.

Towards the end of the week she was reaching breaking-point.

From the moment Sam woke up and went to school, and from the moment he returned from school and went to bed, he talked of nothing but rats. He followed Mother from room to room, and out into the garden when she went to hang washing, reading from books about rats, or from yet another essay he had written about *Rattus rattus*.

When he wasn't reading aloud, he was pointing out how pleased his teachers were with his improved writing and spelling, and how they were amazed that his new-found interest had so drastically improved his school work.

He talked of experts in the field hailing a new boy genius (eventually), and how most experts had their parents to thank for the encouragement and support the parents had given in their formative years. He hinted darkly at young minds being twisted, and brilliant works being thwarted by unsympathetic parents.

Mother was in such a state by Thursday, she began to imagine even darker hints.

She suspected blackmail.

It was in this frame of mind that Mother finally succumbed.

Sam was reading from one of the new rat books that Father had bought him.

Mother could take no more.

She interrupted Sam in the middle of a discourse on mating.

'Sam,' she said, 'I'm going to Sainsbury's.'

Sam hated Sainsbury's.

'I'll come with you,' said Sam, 'and read you the rest of this chapter.'

'It's all right, Sam,' said Mother, 'I can manage on my own. I only need a few things.'

'We're out of cat food,' said Sam. 'Those tins are heavy, not like rat food. I'll come and carry them for you.'

'It's really not necessary, dear,' said Mother.

Sam, taking the shopping basket, noticed Mother's defeated look, and with the generosity of the victor over the vanquished, felt he should say something kind.

'That's a nice pair of shoes you're wearing,' he said, as they walked to the shop. 'I haven't seen them before. Are they new?'

Mother nodded guiltily.

'Does Dad like them?' asked Sam.

'He hasn't seen them yet,' said Mother, who'd been hiding them in a cupboard until the appropriate time came for her to tell Dad she'd had them for ages.

'You ought to wear them when he comes home,' said Sam. 'He'll like them. They're the same colour as his Great Western locomotive.'

'I don't want to wear them out,' said Mother.

'No,' said Sam. 'They look a bit expensive. Rats are cheap,' he added.

Mother stopped walking and looked at Sam.

'Sam,' she sighed, 'I give in. I'll ask Dad if you can have a rat.'

'Mum said she'd talk to Dad tonight,' said Sam.

'Well done!' said James, turning his record-player down. 'How did you manage it?'

Sam frowned. 'I'm not sure,' he admitted. 'I went on about how rats had changed my life, and how I couldn't live without one, all the usual stuff. I was saving the starving myself for a final assault, but she suddenly went all funny when I admired her shoes, and said she'd talk to Dad.'

James shook his head. 'Strange,' he murmured. 'I know Mum is mad about shoes, but I can't see the connection with rats!'

R·H·D·R
Request the pleasure
of your company
at the naming
of the Locomotive
THE ROMNEY
HYTHE & DYMCH
...

4
The Invitation

Father was breathless with excitement when he came home.

'Guess what?' he said. 'The most amazing thing has happened. You won't believe it!'

'Oh,' said Mother, wondering if they'd won the pools, 'what's that?'

'I can hardly believe it myself,' Father chuckled. 'It's incredible!'

He paused, while Mother gazed at him expectantly. 'I've been invited to the naming of a

British Rail locomotive!' he cried triumphantly.

'Oh!' said Mother, who didn't know what else to say.

Father was in such a state of elation, she wondered if she should slip in the fact that she'd just bought another pair of shoes on his credit card, but then remembered she'd promised Sam she would mention the rat. She didn't dare risk both statements at once.

'Sam wants a rat,' she said, but Father was shouting up the stairs for James and Sam to come down and share the good news, and he didn't hear her.

She decided to leave it for the moment.

'They're not in,' said Mother, but Father was dashing towards the telephone, having temporarily forgotten about his sons.

'Must ring John Mawby,' he said. 'He won't believe it either. It's such an honour,' he breathed.

Mother pondered on this, while he chatted excitedly on the phone to his old school friend and fellow train enthusiast.

'What shall I wear?' asked Father when he'd put the phone down.

'For what?' asked Mother.

'For the naming ceremony,' said Father jubilantly.

Mother hesitated. 'I'm not sure,' she answered.

It seemed to her there wasn't much choice — as Father, who had no interest in clothes at all, possessed only one suit.

'I wouldn't go in jeans,' she ventured. 'Perhaps you'd better go in your suit.'

'Good idea!' said Father. 'And I'll wear my white shirt.'

Father sat down in his favourite chair with such a look of bliss on his face, Mother decided the time was ripe.

'I'll take your suit to the cleaners, dear,' she said, 'and take your black shoes to be heeled. And I'll sew a button on your white shirt. You'll have to look smart on such an important occasion.'

Father was delighted and surprised at the warmth of Mother's tone. She hated sewing. In fact she'd hidden his white shirt at the bottom of the laundry basket, hoping Dad would forget about it and buy a new one, complete with buttons.

Normally Father's instinct would sense Mother was up to something, and normally Mother wouldn't be that obvious. But Mother had gauged Father's mood correctly.

'Thank you, dear,' he said, smiling contentedly at his invitation. 'That would be nice.'

He patted Mother's hand, and Mother, encouraged by the gesture, leaned forward and smiled sweetly at Father.

'Darling,' she said, 'don't you think it would be nice if Sam had a little pet rat? He's shown such an

interest in them. His school work has improved drastically, and his teachers are really pleased with his progress. And most brilliant minds,' she added, trying to remember exactly what Sam had said, 'are brilliant because their parents encouraged them in their interests when they were young.'

That didn't sound quite right, thought Mother, but it would have to do.

'He can't possibly have a rat,' said Father calmly. 'We've got two cats.'

'It would be in a cage,' said Mother, 'in Sam's room.'

'That's cruel,' said Father. 'You can't keep an animal caged up all the time.'

'He wouldn't,' said Mother. 'He'd keep his bedroom door closed and let it out every day.'

'But what if someone opens the door,' said Father, 'and Squiffy rushes in? You know what she's like with birds.'

'He could put a big sign on the door saying "Keep Closed At All Times",' said Mother. 'Then no one would open it.'

'The cats can't read,' said Father, pleased with himself.

31

'And they can't open the door when it's closed,' said Mother triumphantly. 'And his bedroom floor is carpeted.'

'I know,' said Father in surprise.

'So it can't slip between the floorboards,' Mother said proudly. 'Let's eat,' she added. 'I've made your favourite treacle tart for pudding.'

'Well?' said James, as Sam wandered into his room.

'He hasn't said yes yet,' said Sam gloomily.

'He will,' said James. 'Just give Mum time.'

'There isn't much time left,' said Sam. 'It's Friday tomorrow.'

'With Mother's treacle tart and a bit of luck, you'll have your rat on Saturday,' said James confidently.

5
A Little Bit of Luck

It was a little bit of luck, rather than the treacle tart that did it.

Dad was waiting in the car the next morning to give Sam a lift to school. He looked at his watch and tooted the horn.

Sam ran out of the house, tripped over a plant pot, and fell headfirst against the apple tree.

Sam was knocked unconscious.

Dad, hearing the crash, jumped out of the car and shouted for Mother.

He carried Sam's limp body through the door that Mother had opened.

Father laid Sam gently on the sofa, while Mother telephoned the doctor with trembling fingers.

James, who had come downstairs on his way to college, saw Father bending over Sam.

'What happened?' he asked in alarm, rushing over to the sofa.

Dad's face was as white as Sam's. 'He ran into the apple tree. The doctor's on his way.'

The colour drained from James's face too, as he knelt down and held Sam's limp hand.

Mother was standing in the doorway, glancing anxiously up and down the street for a sign of the doctor's car.

'Why doesn't he hurry up?' James muttered. 'Why is he taking so long?' He jumped up. 'I'm going to ring him again.'

Just then Sam stirred and James knelt down again.

Father stroked Sam's hair, and Sam opened his eyes.

'Dad,' he murmured weakly, 'can I have a rat?'

6
The Plan

Dad went with Sam on Saturday to collect the rat. Sam had wanted to go on Friday, but Mum wouldn't hear of it and kept him at home, even though the doctor had said that apart from a bruised forehead, Sam seemed none the worse for wear.

So Sam spent Friday looking at the catalogue of cages that Dad had got for him.

Now, as they drove to the pet shop to buy the cage and collect the rat, Sam felt uneasy. In all the excitement he'd forgotten something. He racked his brains for the cause of the unease.

It was something to do with the rat.

As they parked the car, Sam remembered.

He hadn't told his dad that he'd already bought it.

Sam's brain went into overtime.

He needed a plan. He could feign a headache. Dad would drive him home. He could suffer a relapse, admit in his delirium that he'd already bought the rat, and all would be forgiven. But then Dad would call the doctor. He scrapped that plan. He could run into the pet shop before Dad and swear the pet-shop lady to secrecy, but that was too complicated. Arrangements would have to be made for the refunding of his fifty pence, and there was no guarantee that Dad wouldn't wander up to them in the middle of negotiations.

Sam decided he'd have to resort to confusion. He didn't like to; it was too messy, and a lot of luck was involved. But he didn't have time to develop a more sophisticated plan.

The pet-shop lady beamed at Sam as they

entered the shop. He'd tried sneaking in behind his father, but she'd spotted him.

'Hello, young man!' she said. 'Your rat awaits you!'

'Good morning,' said Sam formally, trying to look as though they'd never met before. 'We would like to look at some cages first.'

'How on earth did she know we were planning to buy a rat?' Father whispered, as the lady followed them past the fish tanks towards the rat cages.

Sam pulled the catalogue out of his pocket. 'Perhaps she saw this,' he whispered back.

Father, who had agreed with Sam that the bigger the cage, the happier the rat, was pointing at a gleaming, two-storeyed contraption.

'I was only saying to Peter, my assistant,' said the pet-shop lady as she lifted the cage down for Father to inspect, 'that the minute I set eyes on this young man, I could tell he loved rats. Mind you,' she added, nudging Sam, 'I think your rat knows he's going to a good home. He's only bitten two customers this morning.'

Father, who'd decided he'd had enough sales patter, was getting slightly exasperated. 'Look here,' he protested, 'you're preaching to the converted. My son has already decided to have a rat. You don't have to sell him on the idea.'

Sam winced as the lady smiled fondly at him. 'Oh, I know that,' she said. 'In fact—'

'We wouldn't be buying a cage otherwise would we?' interrupted Sam, hoping he didn't sound rude.

'And I must say you've chosen the best one in the shop,' said the pet-shop lady. 'You'd have to save an awful lot of fifty pences to buy this one,' she added, tweaking Sam's cheek. 'It's funny, isn't it?' she continued. 'You pay fifty pence for a rat, and can end up paying as much as fifty pounds to house it.'

Father, who didn't find it particularly funny, was getting impatient.

'Come on, Sam,' he said. 'Get the bits you need, then we can pay. I don't want to get a parking ticket.'

'And we mustn't forget your rat, young man,' the pet-shop lady added.

She put on a thick glove, and lowered her hand into a cage full of rats. A pinkish-grey rat leaped at her hand. 'Here he is,' she said. The rat embedded its teeth into the glove and was hanging on to the material, swinging from side to side. 'He's a lively little chap,' she said, wriggling her other hand into a glove. To Sam's delight — and Father's distaste — she managed to detach the rat and drop it into the new cage.

'Are you sure that's the one you want?' Father asked. The rat narrowed its eyes and glared at Father. 'It's teeth are yellow.'

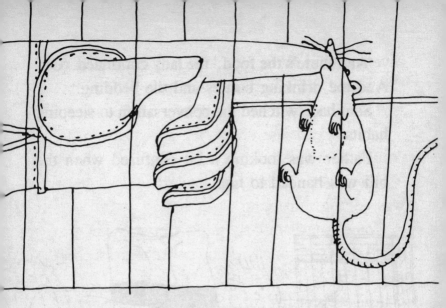

'All rats have yellow teeth,' said the lady cheerfully. 'It's quite normal and healthy! Now, let me see,' she said, producing a calculator.

Sam, who had been gazing at the rat in delight, held his breath. This was the tricky bit.

He started talking.

'There's the cage,' said the pet-shop lady, pressing buttons.

Sam was talking earnestly to Father about diets.

'And there's the food,' the lady continued. 'Oh! And the drinking bottles and the bedding.'

Sam had switched the conversation to sleeping habits.

Father was looking a bit confused when the bill was handed to him.

Sam looked outside as Father started to check the bill.

He couldn't believe his luck. A traffic warden

was moving up the street towards Father's car. 'Hurry up, Dad,' said Sam. 'Traffic wardens!'

Dad looked up from the bill, glanced at the total, and handed the lady some money.

Sam pulled Father towards the door, clutching the cage to his chest. Father grabbed the rest of the packages, still holding the receipt in his hand. He glanced at it and stopped. He turned to the pet-shop lady, who had followed them to the door.

'The rat doesn't seem to be on the bill,' he said.

'Well it wouldn't, would it?' the lady laughed. 'I only charged for the cage, the bottles, the food and the bedding.'

Sam started dragging his father's arm. 'Come on, Dad,' he said, 'he's getting closer!'

'Well,' Father called over his shoulder, 'thank you very much!'

'Yes, thank you!' Sam shouted.

'Enjoy your rat!' the lady shouted back.

Sam and Father managed to get to the car before the traffic warden.

'Perhaps I misjudged the pet-shop lady,' said Father, turning on the engine. 'It was very nice

43

of her not to charge for the rat.' He frowned. 'Although I didn't care for all that heavy sales talk, especially when it's directed at young people. Adults are different, they can see through things. Young people are vulnerable,' he continued, 'and shouldn't be pressured into buying things. They may end up buying things they don't really want.'

'I wouldn't do that, Dad,' said Sam, smiling at the rat on the back seat.

Father looked at Sam's innocent face and frowned again.

'But she wasn't trying to sell you a rat,' he murmured thoughtfully. He chewed his upper lip. 'What I can't understand,' he added, 'is why she was so anxious to *give* you a rat.'

Sam glanced at his father who was deep in thought.

'Dad,' he said, 'let's think of some names.'

7

Rat Phobia

Sam decided to call his rat Nibbles.

Father, noticing the drops of blood and Band-Aid wrappers that made a trail from Sam's room to the bathroom and back, thought Dracula would be more suitable.

Mother and Father were standing by the cage sucking their fingers.

The cats, Bill and Squiffy, indignant at having been locked out of Sam's room, were furiously scratching at the door to be let in.

45

James had popped to the shop for more Band-Aids. Having used up the supply in the bathroom, Sam's friends, who'd been at the house to see Nibbles, had gone home for lunch.

Sam, whose warning to his parents came too late, opened the top of the cage.

'Never put your finger in the cage,' he said. 'He thought you were giving him food. Look,' he added, having taken the precaution of slipping on one of Mother's gardening gloves before lifting the rat out.

He removed the glove and Nibbles ran up his arm and on to his shoulder, where he sat, washing his whiskers.

'Oh!' said Mother, tentatively stroking the soft fur. 'Isn't he sweet?'

'That's not the word I would use,' said Father, looking at his punctured finger.

'Oh!' Mother started guiltily as the doorbell rang. She'd forgotten she had invited their friend Veronica around. 'That must be Veronica, she rang yesterday in quite a state. She didn't say what was wrong,' she added, cautiously opening the bedroom door and grabbing the cats who

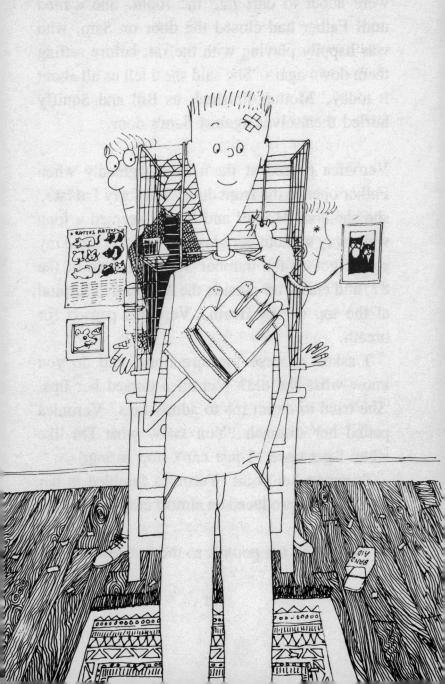

were about to dart into the room. She waited until Father had closed the door on Sam, who was happily playing with the rat, before setting them down again. 'She said she'd tell us all about it today,' Mother finished, as Bill and Squiffy hurled themselves against Sam's door.

Veronica peered at them short-sightedly when Father opened the front door. 'I'm sorry I'm late,' she shouted. Mother and Father seemed a long way away without her glasses. 'I couldn't find my specs, got on the number 37 bus instead of the 87, and ended up outside the Maternity Hospital at the top of the Heath,' Veronica paused for breath.

'I asked a nurse for directions, and do you know what she did?' Veronica pursed her lips. 'She tried to direct me to admissions.' Veronica patted her stomach. 'You know what I'm like when I get upset, I just can't stop eating.'

To prove her point, Veronica fumbled in her handbag and produced an almost empty packet of peanuts.

'I've put on ten pounds in the last few weeks,'

she said, pushing the tempting packet back into her bag. 'I must go on a diet.'

Mother and Father ushered their friend into the front room. They'd never seen her in such a state.

'Whatever's the matter?' Mother asked in concern as Veronica sank on to the sofa.

Veronica sighed. 'I know you're going to think

I'm silly,' she said, 'but I'm going to have to move from my flat.'

'You can't do that,' said Mother, aghast. 'It's a wonderful flat and you've just had it redecorated!'

Veronica sighed again. 'I know. But they're knocking down the building next to it.'

She felt in her bag and produced a handkerchief.

'And I suppose they're going to put up a concrete skyscraper instead,' Father sympathized.

Veronica twisted the handkerchief between her fingers. 'No,' she answered, 'in fact they're going to make a nice little park there.'

'Then why on earth are you thinking of moving?' asked Father.

Veronica's voice faltered. 'It's difficult to explain,' she said. 'You'll think I'm mad.'

'What you need,' said Mother firmly, 'is a medicinal brandy.' She crossed to the sideboard and poured a large measure for their friend.

'The noise must be terrible,' Mother said, handing the drink to Veronica.

'It's not the noise,' said Veronica, taking a sip

from the glass. 'I'm usually at the office when they're working.'

'The dust and grit must be a nuisance,' said Father.

Veronica shook her head. 'That doesn't bother me,' she said, knotting the handkerchief into a ball. She lowered her voice slightly. 'The doctor's put me on tranquillizers. I've been having terrible nightmares since I saw it. I'm convinced they're going to move into my flat. I know it's irrational, and I only saw one. That was the day the bulldozers arrived. And I quite like mice, you know,' Veronica's voice rose hysterically. 'And I'm very fond of hamsters, and they're even bigger. The doctor said it was a phobia, and do you know what else he said?' she took another sip of brandy and shuddered. 'He said if I could force myself to handle one, I would probably lose my fear.' She gulped the remaining brandy. 'Can you imagine,' she cried, gazing roughly in the direction of Mother and Father, 'anything more horrendous?'

'More horrendous than what?' asked Father, bewildered.

'Than handling a rat,' Veronica whispered, as the door opened, and Sam walked in holding Nibbles.

Veronica made an effort to pull herself together. 'Hello, James!' she shouted, smiling bravely as she squinted across the room.

'I'm afraid it's Sam,' said Mother weakly.

'I've brought Nibbles to show you,' said Sam proudly.

'Oh!' cried Veronica, as Mother and Father watched helplessly. 'How lovely! A baby hamster! We were just talking about hamsters.'

'Yes, Sam,' Mother interrupted, 'it's a pet hamster.'

'Yes,' repeated Father, 'a lovely baby *hamster*.'

Sam shrugged. Something in the tone of his parents' voices warned him not to argue.

Veronica jumped up, and before Mother or Father could stop her, started stroking Nibbles. 'Oh! He's gorgeous?' she cried. 'Such a lovely soft coat. And his whiskers tickle!' she exclaimed delightedly.

She rushed back to the sofa again, and felt for her handbag. 'I have a few peanuts left,' she said,

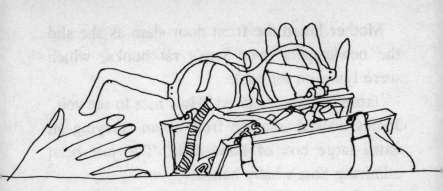

fumbling in the bag. 'I know hamsters love them.'

'Oh, look!' she cried in delight. 'Look what I've found! She held up a pair of spectacles. 'They were in my handbag all the time. Now I can have a really good look at Nibbles.'

Father was pushing Sam out of the door. Mother leaned on the closed door and sighed with relief.

'Oh!' said Veronica, looking through her glasses in disappointment. 'I was hoping to have a proper look at Nibbles.'

'We could hear the cats,' said Mother, inspired by the noise Bill and Squiffy were making as they tried to batter their way out of James's room, where Sam had temporarily placed them.

Mother heard the front door slam as she slid the newspapers over Sam's rat books, which were lying on the table.

'James!' Veronica cried. 'How nice to see you.' James walked into the front room carrying an extra large box of Band-Aids. 'I've just been admiring Sam's baby hamster.'

'I wish I'd known that Nibbles was supposed to have been a hamster,' said James as he went to say goodnight to Sam.

Sam was fixing a wheel into the cage.

'Yes,' said Sam. 'It's a pity Veronica knocked Dad's engine off the shelf when she fainted.'

'Well, at least he managed to mend it,' said James. 'And it was a good idea to make Veronica stroke Nibbles again.'

Nibbles, who didn't seem to know quite what to do with the wheel, sat inspecting it with bright eyes.

'Yes,' Sam agreed. 'I'm glad it cured her phobia.'

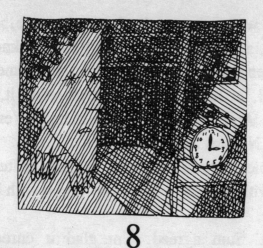

8
Noises In The Night

Mother sat up in the darkness.

It was three o'clock in the morning.

'Wake up!' she hissed, shaking Father.

Father stopped snoring. 'What's wrong?' he murmured sleepily.

'Listen!' Mother held her breath. A strange creaking sound was coming from upstairs.

Father sat bolt upright. The noise stopped. 'It's probably the wind,' he said, falling back against the pillow.

'There it is again!' Mother clutched Father's

arm as the strange noise started up again. 'I think someone is trying to get through the skylight,' Mother whispered nervously. 'It doesn't sound like wind.'

'I'll go and have a look,' said Father, alert now. 'It could be someone after my train collection.'

Mother clutched his arm again. 'I'll go downstairs and ring the police. They might be dangerous.'

Mother tiptoed downstairs, while Father, armed with the water jug, tiptoed upstairs.

They were both glad the landing light was on. Mother had just put the phone down when Father called to her.

Mother picked up a poker, and ran upstairs.

The light was on in Sam's room, and Father stood in the doorway. 'Look!' said Father, pointing with the jug.

The rat froze in its cage and gazed at Mother as she joined Father in the doorway. Then, sliding into the wheel, he started pedalling.

Mother watched mesmerized as the wheel lurched slowly forward, then rolled backwards, then spun furiously in a complete circle,

creaking and groaning under the weight of the rat.

Sam was fast asleep, with his blankets pulled over his head.

'Oh dear!' said Mother, coming out of her trance and heading for the stairs. 'I'd better call the police again.'

Father dropped the water jug when Mother screamed.

Sam sat bolt upright in bed.

James's bedroom door flew open, and Bill and Squiffy bolted downstairs. James stumbled on to the landing.

'What is it?' Father shouted in alarm, rushing up to Mother with Sam behind him.

'I saw a face,' Mother whispered, staring up at the skylight. 'Oh!' she shuddered. 'It was horrible.'

'I'll ring the police,' said James.

'I'll come with you,' said Sam.

'I already have,' Mother said faintly, as the doorbell rang.

Father led the procession downstairs.

'Good evening, sir,' said the police sergeant

standing on the step. 'I'm Sergeant Pattison. I believe you heard strange noises coming from the direction of the skylight.' He pulled a notebook out of his pocket as Mother closed the door.

'Yes,' said Father, 'but—'

'I saw his face,' Mother interrupted. 'It was awful!'

'I've sent one of my officers to have a look

around,' said the sergeant. 'Perhaps you could give me a description of this person.'

'Well,' said Mother, 'he had an evil look in his eyes, although he seemed a bit surprised when I screamed. He had straggly eyebrows,' she added. 'Oh! And very big ears. And a droopy ginger moustache.'

The doorbell rang again as the sergeant finished writing.

'Excuse me,' he said, opening the door, 'this is my colleague, Constable Smith.'

Mother's hand flew to her mouth. A police officer with very big ears, straggly eyebrows and a ginger, droopy moustache was framed in the doorway.

'I'm sorry if I alarmed you, madam,' he said. 'I climbed up the apple tree to get to the roof. There's no sign of an intruder,' he added, as the sergeant looked down at his notebook, then up at Constable Smith.

Father, James and Sam looked at Mother. Mother blushed, 'Well,' she said, 'it's like this . . . Sam has a rat.'

'And it has a squeaky wheel,' Father volunteered

narrowing his eyes at Sam, who was sneaking back upstairs.

The police constable looked bewildered.

'May I suggest, sir,' said Sergeant Pattison, sighing and closing his book, 'that you oil it.'

9
Dad's Big Day

Father's big day finally arrived.

He'd hardly slept all night, and it wasn't Nibbles's wheel that had kept him awake. He'd made sure that Sam oiled it regularly after the incident with the policemen.

It was excitement that had prevented him from sleeping.

It was the morning of the locomotive naming ceremony.

He glanced with satisfaction at the wardrobe

where his suit hung, fresh from the cleaners. His mended shoes, shiny with polish, rested underneath.

Mother was fast asleep. It was seven o'clock on a Sunday morning.

Father wanted to share his excitement. He tossed and turned, adjusted the bedclothes, and beat his pillows into different shapes.

But Mother continued sleeping.

He pretended to be talking in his sleep, twitching his arms and legs as though in the middle of a violent nightmare, but still Mother slept.

So Father, who occasionally suffered from a bad chest, had a coughing fit.

Mother opened one eye, narrowed it at Father, then quickly closed it again.

But Father had spotted the movement.

'I can't sleep either,' said Father. 'I've had a really inspired idea,' he continued happily, pretending he hadn't noticed Mother pulling the quilt over her head.

'I've decided not to take my invitation with me. My name will be on the official guest list so I don't really need to. Besides,' he went on, 'they might keep it and I want to have it framed. It would look marvellous hanging above my trains.'

Mother's muffled voice filtered through the quilt. 'What time is it?'

Father thought he'd better ignore that question. 'I want to allow plenty of time to get ready,' he said. 'I think I'll put my red spotted handkerchief in my breast pocket. Or do you think a flower would be nicer?'

Father thought that by asking a question, he was more likely to get a response.

Mother gave up the idea of a lie-in, as the cats, hearing voices, were scratching at the bedroom door, waiting to be fed.

'I think a flower would be very nice,' Mother answered, climbing out of bed. She knew that the red spotted handkerchief was still waiting to be washed.

'But then I do like my spotted handkerchief,' Father demurred. 'It reminds me of my grandfather. He used to have a handkerchief like that.'

'I think a little rosebud would be nicer,' said Mother. 'There are some lovely buds on the bush your grandmother gave us. Do you remember how much she loved roses?'

'Yes,' Father agreed, smiling at the memory of his grandmother's rose garden. 'Yes,' he repeated, 'I think a rosebud would be very appropriate.'

Mother went downstairs, trying not to trip over the cats, who were rubbing themselves against her legs.

Father had offered to come down and make tea, but Mother, who wasn't awake enough for long conversations about trains, persuaded him to take his bath first, while she sewed a button on his white shirt.

Mother put food down for the cats and looked for the sewing-basket. She tried to remember when she'd last used it. She vaguely remembered trying to sew Sam's Cub Scout badges on to his sweater, but that was over two years ago.

Mother was still searching for the basket when Sam came down.

He was carrying a box of dog biscuits, a packet of parrot seed, and a plastic bag of what looked like grass seed. A book on house pets was clenched between his teeth. He dropped the book on the draining-board and opened it.

'Good morning,' said Mother, who had discovered the sewing-basket in Father's work-room. 'You're up early.'

Sam was engrossed in his book.

'Good morning,' he replied absently. 'Have we got any stale bread?'

Mother knew she had plenty, as she'd forgotten to get fresh bread yesterday. 'There's some in the breadbin,' she said, sitting down at the kitchen table and spreading Father's white shirt across it.

Sam lifted the bread out of the bin, inspected it, and carefully cut the mouldy bits off.

Mother watched as Sam put the dog biscuits and the stale bread into the blender. 'I'm making rat food,' he explained. 'There's a recipe in my household pet book. It says it's very nutritious,' he added, glancing at the book again, 'and very good for their bowel movements.'

'That rat is getting fatter and fatter every day,' said Mother. 'I think you might be overfeeding him.'

'He does eat a lot,' Sam admitted. 'I can't seem to fill him up. Anyway, it says in the book that they will only eat as much as they need.'

'Well,' said Mother, as Sam added the rest of the ingredients to the mixture. 'I think you should put him on a diet before he explodes.'

'I'll just give him half a cup,' said Sam, pouring some of the mixture into a breakfast cup. He tipped the rest into a plastic container, screwed the lid on, then went back upstairs.

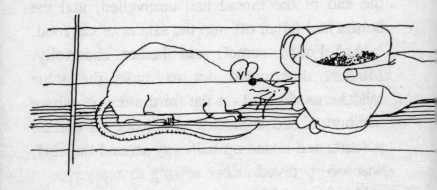

Mother was still having trouble with the button when Father came down an hour later. 'I thought I'd have my cereal before getting dressed,' he said. Father was still in his dressing-gown. 'Where's the muesli?' he asked, looking in the cupboard where it was usually kept.

'I think it's been eaten,' said Mother, concentrating on her fifth attempt at sewing a button on to the cuff of Father's white shirt.

She thought that she'd managed it the first time, but when she had cut the thread she realized she'd sewn both cuffs together and had to start again.

On the second attempt, the knot she'd put on the end of the thread had unravelled, and the button had fallen off into the saucer of cat food.

'Ah! Found some!' said Father cheerfully. Mother, determined not to make the same mistake as she had on the third attempt, where the button had somehow slid from its correct position and ended up half-way around the cuff, was too involved in her sewing to reply.

Her finger still hurt from the last effort, when she'd lost patience with the shirt and stabbed maliciously at the button, which shifted slightly, deflecting the needle into her left index finger.

Fortunately the drops of blood had only stained the shirt-tail, which Father would be tucking into his trousers anyway.

'This is excellent muesli,' Father was saying. 'Better than the one you usually buy.'

Mother gazed at the needle in her hand. The thread from the needle was still attaching the button to the shirt, but something was wrong. She looked down at the table drawer. The thread

had wrapped itself around the knob. If she cut the thread near the button, the button would fall off, as it was attached by only two stitches. If she cut the thread by the needle, there was a good chance the button would shift to the wrong position.

Mother decided to unwind the thread from the knob. This wasn't easy, as the needle kept getting in the way, and the thread, instead of getting longer, was getting shorter.

The needle embedded itself into the wooden table as Mother struggled to free her hand, which had got tangled up with the thread and was now attached to the drawer handle.

'I'd better get dressed in a few minutes,' said Father, refilling his cereal bowl. 'I have to leave at eleven o'clock.'

Mother managed to cut herself free with the nail-scissors, which was difficult with a sore left hand, but Father's shirt was still sewn to the table.

'Gosh!' said Father. 'I've eaten all the muesli. You must get some more of that brand.'

He glanced at Mother, who was studying the

shirt on the kitchen table. 'Don't bother sewing a button on that shirt,' he said. 'I never really liked the cut of the collar. I bought a new one last week.'

Father had already left by the time Sam came back down to the kitchen.

Mother was standing by the table ripping the white shirt to shreds.

'Look!' said Sam, holding up the empty cup. 'He ate every scrap of it. He loved it.' He looked at the plastic container on the sink. 'Oh!' he added with a puzzled frown. 'What happened to the rest of my rat food?'

James was helping Sam construct a tunnel for Nibbles when Father arrived home.

They heard the door slam, an unintelligible shout, and the sound of footsteps racing upstairs.

'We need one more,' said Sam, looking at the construction of toilet-roll tubes sellotaped together.

Father's frustrated cry drifted down the stairs.

'He needs some lavatory paper,' said Mother, who was preparing supper.

'Good,' said Sam, taking the paper that Mother handed him to take up to his father. 'That means there's an empty roll in the bathroom.'

James was shaking with laughter. 'It also means,' he gasped, 'that the recipe in your book was right!' He wiped the tears of laughter from his eyes. 'Your rat food,' he spluttered, 'must be very good for the bowels.'

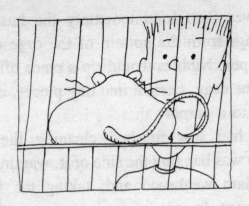

10
Fat Rat

Sam's rat got fatter and fatter.

However much food Sam gave it, it always wanted more.

It even took to stealing Sam's buttered toast when it was out of the cage, and would sit, staring at Sam, defiantly munching it.

Nibbles's shape resembled a large, squashy pear, even though Sam had attempted to put it on a diet.

Nibbles also developed a passion for newspaper.

Whenever Sam tried to empty the husks and droppings from the bottom of the cage on to a newspaper, Nibbles would rip a piece off, carry it into the cage, chew it into tiny pieces, and pile them into a corner.

Sam had just finished cleaning the cage. Nibbles was banging the side of it, wanting more food. Sam weakened and, taking the feeding bowl, went downstairs.

He tiptoed past the front room. Dad was measuring his invitation to the naming ceremony. He was preparing a frame for it, and Sam didn't want to get involved in another conversation about Father's day at the ceremony. Dad hadn't stopped talking about it all week.

Mother was in the kitchen feeding the cats.

Sam went to the bathroom and came back carrying a plastic container that had been hidden in the back of a cupboard.

'Don't forget to put it back when you've finished with it,' said Mother, nodding at the new batch of rat food that Sam had made. 'I had to tell your Father that it's unavailable in the shops and that I couldn't remember the name of the manufacturer. He wanted to write to them and complain about the poor distribution of their muesli.'

She watched as Sam carefully measured some of the food into the bowl.

'That rat is absolutely enormous,' she said. 'I thought you'd put him on a diet.'

'I have,' said Sam, selecting from the fruit bowl the expensive kiwi fruit that Mother was saving to decorate the meringues she was planning to make. 'I'm giving him more fruit. He doesn't seem to lose any weight, though,' he added, taking the avocado that Mother had planned to put in the salad.

'That rat eats better than we do,' Mother observed, as Sam chopped the avocado and added it to the bowl, squeezing the exotic kiwi fruit over the mixture.

Father was moving about in the front room. He'd taken the measurements of the invitation and was heading for his workroom to make a frame.

Sam managed to get the rat food back into its

hiding place, just as Father wandered into the kitchen.

Father was in a good mood.

'It's such a lovely day,' he said to Mother. 'Why don't we go for a drive in the country this afternoon? We can have dinner at that nice little restaurant opposite the miniature railway. James can keep an eye on Sam,' he added.

Sam, who didn't need anyone to keep an eye on him, took the bowl and went into the front room. Yesterday's newspapers were scattered across the table. Sam scooped them up with his free hand and took them upstairs for Nibbles.

James, who liked to sleep at weekends, had only just got up when Father called to them.

'See you later,' he shouted. 'We'll ring you from the restaurant to check that everything is all right.'

'There's mince in the fridge,' Mother called. 'You can make yourselves spaghetti.'

Sam and James shouted goodbye down the stairs.

James yawned and stretched, looking into Sam's room.

R.H.D.R.

Request the pleasure of your company at the naming of the locomotive

ROMNEY HYTHE & DYMCHURCH

TH—

—R

GRAIN SALES

ROCKET IN

HAMPSTEAD

THE SUNDAY

BRITISH RAIL
REINSTATE
THE NAMING
LOCOMOTIVES

'What's Nibbles chewing?' he asked.

'Newspaper,' Sam replied. 'He likes to make a nest out of it.'

'It looks more like cardboard to me,' said James, as Nibbles's sharp teeth sunk themselves into the words '. . . request the pleasure of . . .'

11
The Telephone Call

'What a wonderful afternoon,' said Father in satisfaction as the gates to the miniature railway closed behind them. 'It's a pity they close at seven.'

Mother and Father were the last to leave, and the man at the gate frowned at his watch as he turned the key in the lock.

It was ten minutes past seven.

Mother nodded half-heartedly. 'It's a pity we didn't bring an umbrella as well,' she said, patting her wet hair. They'd been riding on trains all afternoon, and the carriages were open-topped.

'It's only a summer shower,' said Father, who was soaked to the skin. 'We'll soon dry out over dinner.'

They walked across the road to the restaurant, trying to avoid the puddles that had formed on the pitted country road.

Mother and Father relaxed over their meal. The service was slow but the food was good, and as they were in no particular hurry, they didn't mind that it was nine o'clock before the waiter had finished serving them.

'I'll just ring the boys to check they're all right,' said Mother, as Father called for the bill, 'and let them know we're on our way home.'

James answered Mother's phone call.

'Is everything all right?' Mother asked.

'Yes,' replied James.

'Did you have spaghetti?'

'Yes.'

'Was it good?'

'OK.'

'How's Sam?'

'Fine.'

James wasn't very communicative on the telephone.

'We'll be home in about an hour,' said Mother.

'All right,' said James. 'Goodbye.'

Mother was just about to replace the receiver when she heard muffled cries in the background. 'What's that?' she asked anxiously, as the cries grew more clamorous.

'It's Sam,' said James. 'Shouting from upstairs. Hang on — I'll go and see what's wrong.'

Mother pressed the receiver to her ear. She could

hear Sam shrieking, then James's excited voice, then the sound of footsteps and doors banging.

'Hello, hello!' Mother cried into the telephone, willing her voice to be heard through the pandemonium. She shouted into the phone for what seemed like an eternity, wincing at the panicky cries that drifted through the receiver.

Then the receiver suddenly clicked.

There was silence. Then a mournful, high-pitched buzz.

'What's wrong?' asked Father, who had settled the bill and had come to see why Mother was taking so long.

'Something terrible has happened!' Mother whispered. She handed the phone to Father.

'Someone's left it off the hook,' he said.

'That was James!' Mother cried. 'Something awful happened to Sam, and he went upstairs. There was all this dreadful shouting, and then the line went dead.'

'Oh dear!' said Father, trying not to panic as well. He replaced the receiver, then dialled again with trembling fingers.

The same high-pitched buzz came down the line. Father slammed the phone down.

'It's pointless reporting a fault on the line,' he said, thinking quickly. 'It will take time to get it fixed. I know,' he added, 'you ring Hampstead Police. Tell them to go round as fast as they can. I'll get the car and we'll be home in half an hour,' he promised grimly, running towards the door.

They were home in twenty-five minutes. The front room was in darkness as they fumbled with the key.

'There's a light on in Sam's room,' Mother whispered as they crept up the stairs, afraid of what they might find.

Father pushed Sam's door open.

Sam was slumped against a chair, his eyes half closed and his face as white as chalk. James was bending over him with a cup of sweet, strong tea in his hand.

'Oh!' cried Mother, rushing towards them. 'What happened?'

A blissful smile illuminated Sam's face. 'Nibbles has had nine babies,' he said.

12
'Quiet Please!'

Sam was in no fit state to go to school the next day.

The birth had exhausted him.

So Mother let him have a lie-in while she went to the police station to apologize.

She had to face Sergeant Pattison again, but he was very nice about it, considering.

Even Father, who had spent the night sticking his invitation back together, hadn't the heart to be angry with Sam. Anyway, as Mother pointed out, it wasn't entirely Sam's fault. Father shouldn't have left it lying on top of the old newspapers.

'I hope he feels all right today,' said James as he was preparing to leave for college.

'Who?' said Mother. 'Nibbles?'

She still couldn't think of Nibbles as a 'she'.

'No,' said James, 'Sam. He was in a terrible state yesterday. It took me hours to calm him down. He kept running in and out of his room, shouting "another one". When it got to eight,' James continued, 'he nearly fainted!'

'It was nice of Sergeant Pattison to make him a cup of tea,' Mother murmured.

'Yes,' agreed James. 'He said it was good for the nerves, and they always give sweet, strong tea to people in shock.'

Father nodded. Mother had poured him a cup of sweet, strong tea when he'd seen the bits of invitation that James had rescued from Nibbles's cage.

'What are we going to do with all those babies?' Mother asked when James had left to catch the bus. She hadn't told Father yet that she'd already promised Sam he could keep two.

Father frowned. 'They're going to the pet shop as soon as they're old enough,' he said. 'Imagine selling a child a pregnant rat!'

'I'm sure they didn't know it was pregnant,' said Mother. 'After all, they thought it was a male.'

Father frowned again. 'I'm not so sure,' he said. 'That woman seemed very anxious to get rid of it. She didn't even charge for it.'

Father looked at his watch. 'I'll have to go to work in a few minutes,' he said. 'I'll just pop up and see that Sam is all right. I don't think he slept at all last night.'

'I'll come up with you,' said Mother, 'and see if he's ready for some food.'

Sams's room was in semi-darkness.

The curtains were still closed.

A night-light glowed softly next to the rat cage, which was draped with Mother's best lace tablecloth. Sam, who had dark circles under his eyes, was kneeling in front of it, reverently holding a corner of the cloth and

peering in. A book on rat care lay open at his feet.

Mother went to draw the curtains, but Sam's stern whisper stopped her.

'Only open them a little bit,' he hissed. 'Too much light might frighten Nibbles!'

Mother did as she was told and crept back to the cage.

'Oh!' she cried, looking into it. 'They're so sweet!'

'Shhh!' Sam put his finger to his lips. 'You must be very quiet,' he whispered. 'It says in the book that if nursing rats are upset they're liable to eat their young.'

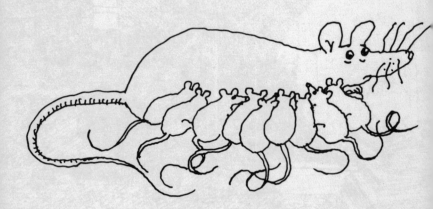

'I'm not surprised,' Father murmured. 'They look like sausages.' He studied the pile of plump pink bodies. 'Raw ones,' he added unnecessarily.

'Isn't it time you went to work, dear?' Mother suggested softly. 'It's nearly ten o'clock.'

Sam, whose mood had shifted from exhaustion to euphoria, followed his father downstairs to say goodbye. Then, as the telephone had been fixed, he telephoned his grandmother in Yorkshire, his aunt in the Midlands and his great-uncle in South Wales.

He could hardly wait for his friends to get out of school to tell them the good news.

Then he busied himself in his bedroom.

He tiptoed around it, tidying things away. He removed the clock-radio so there would be no risk of any sudden noise. He swept the carpet with a soft brush to avoid using the noisy vacuum cleaner, and he taped another notice on the door that said QUIET PLEASE.

13
Victory

Sam's mood changed again.

Father was adamant that the young rats must go.

'I think he's suffering from postnatal depression,' said James. 'He won't come out of his room.'

Father concentrated on his newspaper.

'He hasn't eaten for two days, either,' said Mother. She looked at Father reproachfully.

'Father said all the babies had to go. *All* the babies,' she emphasized.

Father lowered the newspaper. 'They're six

weeks old,' he said. 'They're ready to go. Anyway,' he added defensively, 'that poor rat looks worn out. I should think she'll be glad to get rid of them.'

Mother couldn't argue with that.

The young rats, who were quite large now, never left their mother alone. They sat on her, rolled on her, and bounced on her. They chased her round and round the cage all night, making so much noise that even Sam, who would never admit to being kept awake by them, looked exhausted from lack of sleep. There were just too many of them.

Nibbles looked even more exhausted. The sparkle had gone from her eyes, and the gloss from her coat. Even her appetite had suffered.

'And,' warned Father, interrupting Mother's thoughts, 'if they don't go soon we could have a colony of eighty-odd rats in a few months time.'

Dad had been reading the chapter on reproduction in Sam's book.

James and Mother looked at each other. They'd promised Sam they would try one last stand.

'Don't forget Veronica wants one,' said James.

'And Matt, and Daniel,' said Mother.

'That still leaves six,' said Father, closing his

newspaper decisively, 'and they're going to the pet shop on Saturday.'

James glanced at Mother again.

'I think Sam was only hoping to keep three of them,' he murmured.

'That would mean four rats in one cage,' said Father. 'It's out of the question. Besides,' he added, 'the third one would probably feel left out and attack the other two.'

It was Mother's turn to glance at James.

'How clever,' she cried. 'I hadn't thought of that! Two would be much better. Nibbles could cope with two. They could play together and give Nibbles some time to herself.'

'We'll have to make sure they're both females, of course,' said James, 'but Sam's learned how to sex rats now. It must be a terrible thing,' he added, turning to Mother, 'to be a parent and have all your children taken away from you.'

Mother's eyes took on a misty look. 'I can't imagine,' she whispered, 'anything more terrible.'

Father was searching unsuccessfully in his pocket. His handkerchiefs were still waiting to be washed.

Mother tore off a paper towel and handed it to him.

'I'd better get on with my cooking,' she sighed. 'I'm making a treacle tart for supper.'

'Well?' Sam asked eagerly as James burst into his bedroom. 'How did it go?'

'Brilliantly,' James cried. 'You can keep two!'

'That's great!' said Sam, picking up the new book he'd borrowed from the school library. 'Two is perfect. Any more wouldn't be fair to Nibbles. Besides,' he added, 'it will give me more time for my studies.' He held up the book to show James.

'I thought I should widen my interests,' said Sam, as James read the words *Snakes and How to Keep Them*.

snakes
and how
to keep
them